Raising Chickens for Beginners

The Step-By-Step Guide to Raising Happy, Healthy Chickens in Your Backyard | Discover the Secrets to Producing Fresh Eggs and Quality Meat From Your Home Farm

By

Joseph Hammers

© **Copyright 2023 by Joseph Hammers - All rights reserved.**

This document is geared towards providing exact and reliable information in regard to the topic and issue covered. The publication is sold with the idea that the publisher is not required to render accounting, officially permitted or otherwise qualified services. If advice is necessary, legal, or professional, a practiced individual in the profession should be ordered.

From a Declaration of Principles, which was accepted and approved equally by a Committee of the American Bar Association and a Committee of Publishers and Associations.

In no way is it legal to reproduce, duplicate, or transmit any part of this document in either electronic means or in printed format. Recording of this publication is strictly prohibited, and any storage of this document is not allowed unless with written permission from the publisher.

All rights reserved. The information provided herein is stated to be truthful and consistent in that any liability, in terms of inattention or otherwise, by any usage or abuse of any policies, processes, or directions contained within is the solitary and utter responsibility of the recipient reader. Under no circumstances will any legal responsibility or blame be held against the publisher for any reparation, damages, or monetary loss due to the information herein, either directly or indirectly.

Respective authors own all copyrights not held by the publisher.

The information herein is offered for informational purposes solely and is universal as so. The presentation of the information is without a contract or any type of guaranteed assurance.

The trademarks that are used are without any consent, and the publication of the trademark is without permission or backing by the trademark owner. All trademarks and brands within this book are for clarifying purposes only and are owned by the owners themselves, not affiliated with this document.

Table of Contents

Introduction 4

Chapter 1: Why do you keep chickens in your backyard? 6

   1.1 Environmental and health advantages 6

   1.2 Cost savings for food 7

   1.3 Personal satisfaction 8

Chapter 2: The Egg 10

   2.1 What is the meaning of the term fresh farm? 10

   2.2 Store-bought eggs 10

   2.3 Free-range chickens eggs vs. store-bought eggs 11

   2.4 How to gather and keep hen eggs? ... 12

   2.5 Cleaning up chicken eggs 14

   2.6 Preserving chicken eggs 15

   2.7 The process of incubation and the many phases of egg development 15

   2.8 Techniques for incubation 17

   2.9 The significance of incubator cleanliness 19

Chapter 3: Meat 21

   3.1 Chickens: purebred versus hybrid 21

   3.2 How to choose the best chicken breeds for meat production? 22

   3.3 Processing of chicken: timing of slaughter and preparation of flesh 25

   3.4 How to keep raw chicken fresh? 29

Chapter 4: Nutrition 31

   4.1 Why do hens need a well-balanced diet? 31

   4.2 Chicken feed types 32

   4.3 Useful dietary additions for hens 36

   4.4 How to make homemade chicken feed? 37

   4.5 How to stop wasting food 39

   4.6 Calculating chickens' food consumption 39

Chapter 5: The chicken coop 42

   5.1 How to locate a hen house? 42

   5.2 Materials required for construction .. 43

   5.3 The best hen house size and design.. 44

Chapter 6: Chickens' health 47

   6.1 A sick hen's Signs and Intervention.. 47

   6.2 Preventing common diseases 48

   6.3 Poultry house cleanliness is crucial .. 49

Chapter 7: : Self-sustenance 51

   7.1 Food preparation with hen's meat and eggs? 51

   7.2 Recipes using eggs and chicken meat 52

   7.3 Keeping eggs and meat fresh for future use 59

   7.4 Producing fertilizer for the home garden 59

Conclusion 61

Introduction

Raising hens may be relaxing, rewarding, entertaining, and even a little nerve-wracking for novices. It is extremely difficult to determine what information about rearing chicks and chickens is accurate, false, or just plain strange.

A class of domesticated birds known as chickens has long been linked to mankind. Since they were brought up to be farm animals, chickens have been a subject of surprise and wonder, and their meat and eggs have become one of the main sources of protein in the human diet.

Chickens have always had the same fundamental needs: sustenance, protection, and procreation. They were on the planet long before humans. In contrast to the wild ancestors from which they evolved, domesticated chickens rely on humans to provide for their physiological and psychological needs.

Different breeds evolved over the ages for various reasons in various locations. So, modern breeds go from being so little to fit in your palm to be so tall that they reach almost to your waist. It can be found in a wide variety of colors and designs, from basic black, white, blue, and red to polka-dotted patterns, lace, and stripes. The chicken's feathers may be long and thin, wide and short, or fur-like, and they may cover not only its body but also its feet, which resemble boots; its legs, which resemble pants; its beak, which resembles a mustache or a mustache, and its head, which resembles a fancy Easter bonnet.

Some chickens are almost self-sufficient foragers, depending on the features for which these diverse varieties were selected, while others huddle by the trough in anticipation of the next meal. Some people still have a natural sense of self-preservation, while others lack the common sense to get inside when it starts to rain. Not all female chickens share the same maternal instinct or desire to lay eggs and raise chicks. A few kinds of cock still need humans to fertilize eggs in order to generate more of their kind; the majority of cocks still mate in the traditional manner.

Humans, on the other hand, have a variety of needs and desires. Many of us desire meaty chickens that lay an abundance of delicious eggs, grow huge or quickly, or both rapidly and large, while others find nothing more beautiful than brightly colored chickens playing in the sun. Still, others appreciate the simple friendship of these large terrestrial birds.

Our relationships with hens are influenced by the diverse ways we live. There are some of us who live on farms where the chickens have lots of room to wander and nobody to complain to about them. Others reside in densely populated areas, where hens require more vigilant care to prevent them from annoying nearby residents or becoming a tasty snack for neighboring canines.

Due to the enormous differences between chickens and humans, there are countless variations in the reasons people keep chickens, the number of birds they keep, the breeds they choose, and the methods used to care for and protect them. This is why no one can provide you with an absolute guide to chicken raising or tell you exactly how to go about starting your own flock. The most that can be done is to outline the requirements of chickens, suggest various means by which these requirements can be met, and allow you to decide which method is most appropriate for your circumstances.

All the information you'll ever need to know about taking care of your birds, from baby chicks to adult hens, is compiled here for your convenience. Once you have chickens, you won't stop growing or grinning.

In an effort to prevent confusion for you, we have attempted to reduce it to its simplest form. You are urged to read it all the way through.

You should reflect on a few things before getting your chicks or birds:

- Why are they being raised by you? – meat, eggs, or pleasure?
- Do you have a place in mind for them?
- Do you have the time to spend with them?
- When required, are you prepared to "muck out" their coop?
- If you take a trip, who will watch over them?
- Do you have a limit on how many chickens you can own?

Despite the apparent frivolity of these inquiries, many people failed to appreciate the labor and time required to properly care for hens, and the animals suffered as a result.

Chapter 1: Why do you keep chickens in your backyard?

Chickens were previously common family pets, but they have fallen out of favor due to restrictions placed on them by local governments, the fear of rat infestation, and the annoyance caused by their noise and odor.

Chickens are living creatures that have a lot to give the environment and us. They aid in the creation of healthy soil, advance sustainable food production, do away with the necessity for factory-farmed food, and function wonderfully (and naturally) as an insecticide.

Keeping hens at home has a lot of personal benefits in addition to the many environmental advantages. It could be worthwhile to study and pass along these details regarding backyard egg layers if you've been debating getting hens or are attempting to persuade your elected officials to give them a chance.

1.1 Environmental and health advantages

The many environmental advantages of growing hens on a small homestead or in your backyard rather than purchasing your meat and eggs from the highly wasteful industrial, agricultural juggernaut are, however, one that is sometimes overlooked.

The environmental and health benefits of backyard chicken coops are numerous; following, you will find some of the most important ones, as well as how to get the most out of your flock:

- **They work very well as a form of pest control**

Chickens have an insatiable hunger for insects and adore eating grasshoppers, slugs, snails, and beetles, which stops the pests from damaging your plants. Providing your hens with a diet rich in bugs and insects is not only good for their health but will also improve the flavor of your eggs. The chickens get fed, and you get nicer eggs in the morning without resorting to harmful pesticides and chemicals in your garden.

- **They lay more nutrient-dense eggs**

Chickens have the chance to lay more nutrient-dense eggs when they have space to move, forage for insects, and consume higher-quality feed. The omega-3 fatty acids in the eggs from pastureraised and backyard wandering hens are two to three times higher than those from industrial sources, and they have one-third less cholesterol than eggs from factory farms.

- **Your yard is the best place for them**

If you keep your own chickens and eat their eggs, you can help ensure that the hens are healthy and happy. Industrial farms frequently confine their hens in cramped, terrible conditions where they can't move about and eventually grow hostile and sad. You are providing your chickens a higher quality of life by raising them ethically and responsibly, and they will repay the favor.

- **They are wonderful pets**

Your relationship with nature will be strengthened by keeping chickens, which will also help you teach your kids and other family members how to take care of the environment and its inhabitants and demonstrate to them the complete life and feeding cycles of animals. Actually, chickens make wonderful friendly and social pets, and it's so much fun to watch them roam around your yard.

- **They help you remain physically active**

Some people feel healthier when they take care of chickens because it gives them a sense of duty and satisfaction. As chicken keepers frequently spend more time outside working to maintain their coop or just enjoying the company of their feathery friends, the activity also promotes a more active lifestyle.

- **Chicken owners have greater mental health**

Numerous studies have looked at the psychological advantages of owning pets, and don't forget that hens make excellent pets. Researchers discovered that pets:

- Greater self-esteem
- Become more accountable or considerate of others
- Satiate societal demands
- Develop resiliency to cope with social exclusion
- Reduce the negative

1.2 Cost savings for food

People look for alternatives to help lower food costs when food prices rise. But you might want to think about the financial (and emotional) expenses associated with ideas like keeping chickens in your backyard for egg production.

- o **Set your chickens free**

Reduce the cost of your chickens' food by letting them roam free. As natural foragers, chickens will consume grass, bugs, and other vegetation. Their food can be supplemented by this, which will require less feed overall.

- o **Give them table scraps**

Chickens may eat a range of foods and are not picky eaters. Table leftovers like leftover grains, fruit, and vegetable peelings are OK to offer them. Just be cautious not to feed them anything poisonous to chickens, such as avocado or chocolate.

- o **Eliminating egg and meat purchases**

If you raise your own chickens, you won't need to buy meat or eggs from the grocery store. This can add up to significant savings over time.

- o **They aid in producing quality compost and fertilizer for your garden**

Chickens have a very high output of feces. They can expel trash as frequently as 50 times each day! Many people spend a lot of money on bags of organic fertilizer, which is devoid of the chemicals frequently present in manufactured fertilizers, but if you keep hens for your own use, you can always have a supply on hand. Chickens are omnivores. Thus their excrement is devoid of the bacteria and illnesses that are present in that of animals who eat meat. By feeding your chickens an organic diet; you can ensure that your fertilizer is chemical-free as well. Collecting it and applying it to your vegetable patches and garden beds gives your plants an excellent variety of nutrients. Additionally, the grass in your yard will remain fertilized and healthy if you raise hens on a free range.

1.3 Personal satisfaction

A sense of fulfillment and personal satisfaction are just a few advantages of keeping hens in the garden. People may decide to keep chickens in their backyard for a variety of reasons, including:

- o **Food self-sufficiency**

People can create their own food by keeping chickens in the backyard, which can be a fulfilling experience. Additionally, this may lessen dependency on processed foods, which is advantageous for the environment and human health.

- **Educational experience**

Both adults and children can learn something from raising hens. It might present a chance to pick up knowledge about feeding animals, growing food, and maintaining the environment. Future generations can be taught this information, which will aid in fostering a culture of sustainability and self-sufficiency.

- **Positive social interactions**

Maintaining hens can be a chance to interact with the neighborhood. Sharing eggs from backyard hens or frequenting farmer's markets are two ways in which people can strengthen their ties to the neighborhood and bond with their neighbors.

Many poultry farmers also display their birds at regional and national fairs because the experience is as much fun as the meat, eggs, and exhibits they produce. Birds' physical attributes, such as their body conformation, color, and feather quality, are scored by judges using a point system.

Many bird keepers find that presenting their birds is a great way to network with other bird lovers all around the country and pick up useful information for raising their own flocks.

- **Backyard Entertainment**

Almost all flock keepers have stories about the unique personalities and traits of their flock members. Even though there are similarities among breeds, flock raisers can easily identify the distinctive characteristics of their birds because each breed of chicken is different. Knowing our birds better makes taking care of them much more fun.

A backyard flock may be entertaining during its whole lifespan, from sitting on the porch and watching the hens to settling the chicks into the brooder.

Chapter 2: The Egg

One of our diets' more adaptable foods is the egg. Eggs are consumed all throughout the world, whether they are fried, boiled, poached, deviled, or scrambled. Eggs provide pasta and baked products structure.

Eggs are a great source of protein, and they also include a wide variety of vitamins (A, B, D, E, and K) and minerals. In order to feed their families with fresh eggs, more people than ever before are raising hens in their own backyards.

If you maintain chickens, you know there's nothing like the taste of a farm-fresh egg or the satisfaction of making something delicious out of these tiny nutritional powerhouses.

2.1 What is the meaning of the term fresh farm?

It's crucial to be specific about the type of farming we imply when we say something is "farm fresh." Although the phrase "free range" conjures up pictures of broad fields, the majority of chicken products sold as such are actually made on factory farms. The food that these free-range hens receive is often the same as that supplied to cage-raised chickens, and they are kept in crowded, stressful conditions.

When we talk about chickens being "farm fresh," we're referring to "pastured hens" that have been kept on small farms with access to outside space.

If you're a small farmer and you decide to keep your own hens for eggs, you'll have the satisfaction of eating eggs that are true "farm fresh," not just "cage-free" or "free range.".

2.2 Store-bought eggs

Most of the eggs found in shops come from hens that are kept in conditions of horrific overcrowding. In actuality, many hens used for commercial egg production never even touch the ground. Instead, they are made to dwell with dozens of other chickens in what seems to be an overcrowded cage, rarely, if ever, experiencing true sunlight.

Eggs laid by chickens can be any hue from black to light brown to pale yellow to pure white. Brown eggs from "free range" hens are frequent, but this doesn't necessarily mean the birds were healthier or wilder; it merely means the breed that lays the eggs is known for producing them.

People frequently believe that "free-range" or "cage-free" hens have better living circumstances and lay nicer eggs. Part of this is because people believe that brown eggs are better for you than white ones. In actuality, neither of these chicken breeds is raised under humane conditions.

Hens that are maintained "cage-free" and "free-range" are both confined indoors. Their meal is an artificially produced mixture of grains and vitamins. As long as the hens are healthy and laying, this is fine, but it's not ideal if you want your eggs to taste amazing. When chickens eat on open grass, they get a lot of stress and don't get enough micronutrients. This makes their eggs less healthy.

2.3 Free-range chickens eggs vs. store-bought eggs

The nutritional value, production circumstances, and freshness of eggs from free-range chickens differ from eggs from conventional hens in a number of ways.

- **Production conditions**

Buying farm-fresh eggs has a number of advantages, one of which is knowing exactly how the birds were bred. Unfortunately, chickens are kept for their whole lives in small cages or cages powered by batteries in the majority of industrial egg farms. Hens hardly get a chance to go outside, and they hardly have space to turn around! Supporting farmers that let chickens forage for their own food and engage in natural behaviors such as scratching in the soil and nibbling on grass is a perk of buying eggs from local farms. Chickens are omnivores and will fight for the last tomato bite as well as worms and other insects.

- **Nutritional differences**

As everyone is aware, "happy cows make healthy milk" also holds true for chickens. It's true that happy hens lay healthier eggs.

Free-range chickens are given unrestricted access to a pasture or yard where they can contentedly roam, gallop, and flap around while searching for tasty morsels to add to their diversified diet, including greens, grass, bugs, and chicken feed. These chickens are in excellent condition thanks to a diet high in nutrients and regular exercise, so it stands to reason that their byproducts would be as well.

Commercial hens are frequently kept in terrible conditions, such as small cages filled with their own waste and with little or no access to the air, sunshine, or grounds that provide them with the vital nutrients they require to remain healthy. Thus it is understandable why they aren't nearly as nutrient-dense as other types of poultry.

When compared to store-bought eggs, studies have found that farm-fresh eggs have:

- a third less cholesterol
- 1/4 less saturated fat
- 33% more vitamin A
- double the amount of omega-3 fatty acids
- three times as much vitamin E
- Four to six times the amount of vitamin D
- a 7-fold increase in beta carotene

When contrasting farm-fresh eggs with store-bought eggs, these findings are the cherry on top.

- **Taste**

Now that your egg has been cracked and looks great, it's time for the true test: the taste test. After trying fresh free-range eggs in any of your favorite recipes, you won't want to go back to store-bought eggs.

The flavor of fresh eggs is far more powerful and full-bodied, whereas the flavor of store-bought eggs is milder and more delicate.

They are extremely wonderful as a dish on their own because farm fresh is the better option, and they will also improve your next pavlova or quiche more than their store-bought counterpart.

- **Shelf life**

The USDA advises keeping eggs in the refrigerator for no more than two weeks because it can be difficult to determine the precise date that they were laid. Eggs from a farm will keep for two weeks if not refrigerated and for three months if they are.

2.4 How to gather and keep hen eggs?

When a chicken lays an egg, it does so and then wanders away. Instead of clucking, a broody chicken will produce a low rumbling sound as it attempts to hatch the eggs. She will also sit fixated on her nest, leaving it to consume food and drink.

You no longer need to feel guilty about collecting your chicken's eggs now that you are aware of the distinction.

Fresh eggs from a farm are considerably more delicious than eggs from a shop. You can't tell when eggs were harvested, how clean the nests were, how well the birds were doing, or how the eggs were cleaned up before being delivered to the store if you buy them at the store.

Making sure your eggs are properly collected, washed, and stored will help them stay nice and fresh for a lot longer.

- **Egg collection intervals**

Nests should always be checked twice daily for eggs.

Eggs that are left in the nest for an excessively long time may fracture or break due to typical nest activity. In the chicken run, you run the risk of developing a really bad habit.

Chickens consume eggs. One of the chickens is bound to find the egg's contents if it breaks, and once they see she's enjoying the treat, the rest of the flock will join her.

The issue is that chickens genuinely possess a high level of intelligence. They rapidly deduce that the egg is the source of the food they've been enjoying, and they begin breaking them as soon as they're laid. They also have amazing memories, so when the chance comes, they will always keep this practice.

On a daily and nightly basis, check your nests for fresh eggs.

How should you gather the eggs?

Feed the chickens first. They will come to understand that you are entering their enclosure signals pleasant things because they are always hungry for something delectable. To eat, they will immediately depart from their nests.

Always begin with the nests where there are no chickens perched on the eggs. The hens on nests will frequently get up as you go from one nest to another and go with their friends to get food.

It's not always a sign of broodiness when a chicken won't leave the nest. She might not even be hungry. Make your choice while keeping in mind the symptoms of a broody chicken.

Chickens who are broody are more possessive and cautious of their eggs. If you're worried about getting bit, it's best to cover up with some long sleeves and pants.

Would you like more chickens?

On average, hens produce one egg daily. The hen can be broody if you discover a nest with many eggs. In the event that you suspect she is broody, gently lift her away from the nest while inspecting the eggs for any damage.

Taking the eggs and returning the hen to the nest gently will prevent the laying of any additional chicks. She'll soon resume laying eggs normally.

Once you have inspected the eggs for breaking and want more chicks, carefully place her back on her eggs. If an egg is fractured or damaged, you must take it from the nest as soon as you notice it, which means checking on it twice a day.

The incubation period for chickens is 20 to 21 days. Do not remove an egg with a crack if you see one around that time because it is likely just hatching.

While hens may produce fewer eggs in the winter, it is important to keep them from freezing by collecting them frequently.

In the summer, eggs exposed to intense heat soon go bad. The nests will need to be checked frequently, and the eggs should be moved to a cool area or kept in the refrigerator.

2.5 Cleaning up chicken eggs

If possible, avoid washing farm-fresh eggs; instead, clean them with a rough, dry cloth. A "bloom," a naturally occurring layer on eggshells, guards the egg against microorganisms. The protective covering is removed when the eggs are washed, necessitating refrigeration. In any other case, the eggs can be kept on the kitchen counter for up to one month, or they can be kept in the refrigerator; the choice is up to the individual.

Remove the eggs if they have some manure on them. Keep the straw clean and remove any large bits of muck, but accept that some dirt will inevitably find its way onto the eggs despite your best efforts. To remove tiny messes, simply wipe with a moist towel.

A vegetable brush and water can be used to scrub a severely soiled egg. Use warm water at all times—warmer than the egg. Cold water will cause the egg to shrink inside its shell and will encourage the growth of bacteria.

Washing the eggs should be done quickly and gently. Before storing eggs, let them fully dry out in the air.

2.6 Preserving chicken eggs

Once the eggs are dry and clean, put them in the egg cartons and write the date that the eggs were gathered on the cartons. Eggs should generally be kept in the refrigerator. Wet-cleaned eggs need to be kept in the fridge, but dry-cleaned eggs that still have their bloom can be kept in the fridge or at room temperature. Generally speaking, all eggs keep better in the fridge.

Here are some guidelines for maintaining eggs.:

- o When kept in the refrigerator, eggs stay fresh for 4 - 5 weeks from the day of collecting.
- o After a month, the eggs might continue to be edible for a few more weeks.
- o Use older eggs in baking or boil them for a long time.
- o Eggs should be washed right away before cooking after being dry-cleaned, which can be done for several weeks.

2.7 The process of incubation and the many phases of egg development

The process through which an egg becomes a chick is one of nature's greatest miracles. After only three short weeks of incubation, a chick is born. That a little germ can be contained in an egg and, in just twenty-one days, grow into a lovely little chick is mind-boggling to me.

It is a minor daily miracle to imagine that this chick would develop into a chubby hen and then lay eggs to carry the flock's genetic lineage.

If the chick turns out to be a rooster, he may one day become the flock's boss and be tasked with looking after the ladies.

You will then concentrate on the stages of egg development:

- o **Egg fertilization**

The first phase of the hen's life cycle begins with fertilization of the egg. When a hen and rooster procreate, the rooster's sperm will make its way to the female's egg and fertilize it.

The Infundibulum, the portion of the reproductive system that comes behind the ovary, is where fertilization takes place. Only about fifteen minutes pass while the egg is in the infundibulum. Thus there is a very tiny window of opportunity.

The egg will be infertile if sperm does not successfully deposit here.

- **Egg development**

At the time of egg laying, embryonic development has progressed a little bit, but it normally halts until the right conditions for the cells are created, at which point incubation can resume. All the cells in an embryo are identical at the start, but as it grows, differences emerge. Some cells may develop into essential organs, while others may become a leg or wing. The highlights of the chick's development for each day of the incubation period are provided below.

- Day 1: The germinal (embryonic) disk begins to form.
- Day 2: Blood circulation and tissue growth begin.
- Day 3: Blood vessels can be seen as the heart begins to beat.
- Day 4: On this day, an amniotic sac begins to form.
- Day 5: During candling, the knees, elbows, and eyes all develop in unique ways.
- Day 6: The initiation of voluntary movement and the formation of the beak.
- Day 7: Comb starts to grow on day 7.
- Day 8: Opening of the ear canals and the formation of feather follicles.
- Day 9: The embryo is beginning to resemble a bird and is developing claws.
- Day 10: The development of egg teeth and claws.
- Day 11: The tail feathers start to sprout.
- Day 12: Feathers start to appear on day 12.
- Day 13: Legs begin to develop, and their bodies are lightly covered in feathers.
- Day 14: The position of the head is pipping.
- Day 15: Chick will eat egg white on day 15.
- Day 16: They now have full-grown feathers.
- Day 17: Their head is now positioned between their knees, and the egg white has been digested.

- Day 18: They are now almost fully grown. The head is snuggled under the right wing with the yolk sac remaining outside the body. If your embryos are currently in the incubator, today is a lockdown.
- Day 19: Yolk sac has entered the body, and the embryo has taken over all but the air cell.
- Day 20: The umbilicus is now closed, and the yolk-sac has digested. Once the embryo starts to breathe air, it develops into the chick. This is the beginning of the pipping!
- Day 21: This is also referred to as "hatch day." Hatching typically takes place in eighteen hours. However, it occasionally takes longer.

Your chicks can remain in the incubator for up to two full days after they hatch. They will get moving quite soon if a broody is handling the situation.

Remember that roosters will probably result from hatching eggs. A chick's chance of being born a rooster is 50/50. It is impossible to see whether a female or male chick is growing inside of an egg. Have a plan for where you will place a rooster if you can't keep him because some town ordinances forbid backyard roosters.

It is advised to retain one rooster if you chose to do so just. Additionally, for sustained breeding, one rooster for every 10 hens is typical. Any less puts the hens at risk of overbreeding and harm.

With the right planning and tools, hatching eggs may be a very gratifying process. Before fertilized eggs arrive, make sure to verify all of your equipment. As hatch day draws closer, set up your brooder.

Invite friends and relatives over to see the hatch while keeping a close check on the incubator's humidity and temperature. Everyone will be riveted by it! Most importantly, cherish the newborn flock members you had the honor of rearing.

2.8 Techniques for incubation

There are two ways that poultry eggs can hatch. These techniques are described below:

1. **Natural incubation**

In natural incubation, the hen or a broody hen (one that has developed maternal tendencies and is ready to sit on eggs to hatch them) incubates the eggs on her own. By sitting on the eggs and turning them frequently to maintain even heating, the hen keeps them warm. Through breathing and supplying moisture to her body, she also controls the humidity level around the eggs. Natural incubation lasts around 21 days, during which time the embryo develops and hatches.

Benefits of natural incubation

- There is no requirement for additional incubator equipment because a broody hen incubates the eggs using her own body heat.

- Incubation of eggs in a natural setting, which may improve the health and vitality of the offspring.

- The hen may adjust the temperature and humidity of the nesting area to ensure that the eggs hatch successfully on their own.

The Drawbacks of Natural Incubation

- Limited capacity: A hen's size and breed will determine how many eggs she can successfully incubate at once.

- Greater duration: Compared to artificial incubation techniques, natural incubation might last up to 21 days longer.

- Unpredictable: Hens occasionally leave the nest or unintentionally damage eggs, resulting in reduced hatch rates.

2. **Artificial incubation**

When eggs are incubated artificially, a piece of specialized machinery known as an incubator is used. Incubators provide a temperature-, humidity-, and ventilation-controlled environment for the development of embryos. To guarantee uniform heating and to keep the embryo from being stuck to the eggshell, the incubator's rotors can be set to turn the eggs automatically or by hand at regular intervals. Artificial incubation lasts for around 21 days as well.

Benefits of artificial incubation

- Greater capacity: Higher hatch rates are possible because of the larger capacity of incubators.

- Environment control: By carefully regulating temperature, humidity, and ventilation, the best conditions possible for embryo growth can be achieved.

- Predictable: The procedure is more dependable, with constant hatch rates as a result.

Drawbacks of artificial incubation

- Equipment cost: Since incubators require electricity and ongoing maintenance, they can be costly to buy and run.

- Absence of a natural environment: Because eggs are not kept in a natural setting, weaker chicks may develop as a result.

- Monitoring is required: Artificial incubation necessitates regular monitoring to guarantee proper temperature, humidity, and ventilation.

2.9 The significance of incubator cleanliness

It's simple to develop poor habits because many people undervalue how important it is to clean your home. However, you must use an egg incubator with the same respect and caution as you would any other tool. In addition to increasing hatch rates, proper cleaning will significantly extend the useful life of your incubator. Cleaning your incubator every day or even every week won't help because it will slow down the process of incubating eggs. But equally, doing it only once a year is useless!

Here are some major arguments for the significance of incubator hygiene:

- **Keeping germs from growing:** Incubators offer a warm, moist atmosphere that may be favorable for bacterial growth. Bacterial growth, if unregulated, has the potential to contaminate eggs and embryos, which would decrease the likelihood of a successful hatch and raise the mortality rate of chicks.

- **Reducing the spread of disease:** Bacteria and other diseases can be transferred from person to person and from surface to surface in an incubator. Diseases brought on by these viruses have the potential to infect eggs and embryos, resulting in high death rates and poor health in the chicks.

- **Promoting healthy hatchlings:** Keeping the incubator clean and sanitary can help the embryos grow in a clean and healthy setting, which can lead to healthy hatchlings. Chicks who hatch in a healthy, disease-free environment have a greater chance of surviving and a higher quality of life.

Here are some guidelines for maintaining good incubator hygiene to prevent the spread of infections and illnesses during incubation:

- **Regular maintenance:** Follow the manufacturer's recommendations and clean the incubator completely both prior to and following each usage. Remove all trash, like eggshells and poop, and use a light disinfectant solution to clean all surfaces, like the walls, trays, and racks. To get rid of any disinfectant residue, thoroughly rinse the area with clean water.
- **Proper ventilation:** It is essential for allowing for fresh air circulation and lowering humidity levels, which can lead to an incubator's ability to foster bacterial growth.
- **Hand hygiene:** Proper hand washing is required before working with eggs, embryos, or the incubator itself. To avoid cross-contamination, handle eggs or embryos with disposable gloves.
- **Egg sanitation:** Prior to putting the eggs in the incubator, clean them. To get rid of any debris or dirt, gently wipe them with a clean, moist cloth. Do not use eggs that have visible contamination or cracks.
- **Equipment sanitation:** Regular cleaning and disinfection of incubation equipment (including trays, racks, and thermometers) is essential for preventing the growth of bacteria and other potentially harmful microorganisms.
- **Monitoring humidity and temperature:** Consistently monitor and maintain the incubator's temperature and humidity levels in accordance with the needs of the species being incubated. Controlling the temperature and humidity in the right way can stop bacteria from growing and help eggs grow and develop in a healthy way.

Chapter 3: Meat

One of the most common options for backyard farms or small homesteads wishing to raise their own meat is hens. However, take some time to educate yourself on the various meat chicken breeds before starting your flock. There are numerous varieties of meat chicken breeds available, each with advantages and disadvantages. Doing your research is crucial before you start parenting them.

Broilers are a typical name for chickens kept solely for their meat. Because they grow more quickly than chickens reared for egg laying and chicks are regarded to be dual-purpose, broilers make excellent meat chickens.

Broilers, or commercial chickens, reach their peak size at 10 weeks of age and are perfect for feeding a family of four. At 5 weeks of age, they weigh about 4 to 5 pounds.

As a result, breeding and keeping broilers in your garden is your best bet if you want to live independently.

3.1 Chickens: purebred versus hybrid

Which breed of chicken best meets your needs should be one of your first and most crucial considerations when considering whether to keep chickens. You can get a sense of the answer by considering whether you want hens as a pet, for display, or as a source of food. For many people, it will be a mix of these, giving you more things to think about before making a choice.

Here are the key distinctions between hybrid and pure-breed animals.

- **Advantages and disadvantages of pure breeds**

Pure breeds offer a wide range of birds, from the textbook New Hampshire Red to ones that look really exotic, like the Silkie with its silky feathers. However, this has both advantages and disadvantages because there are so many breeds, each with a variety of personalities and traits. To be prepared for potential innate behavioral issues, it is crucial to conduct thorough research on the characteristics of particular breeds before making a purchase. The gene pool may be constrained if you choose a particularly unique breed, which could result in genetic health problems.

Pure breeds often have longer lifespans than hybrids, although they may not be as tolerant to environmental extremes and disease resistance. Keepers with more expertise are perhaps best suited to these animals because they may need a little more care to stay in good shape.

While most pure breeds stop producing throughout the winter, hybrids maintain laying year-round, keeping you fed. Some have an amazing 340 egg production every year.

- **Hybrid hype**

Unlike pure breeds, which come in many different shapes and colors, mixes tend to be flat and brown, white, or black. A Goldline or a Rhode Star would be produced if you asked a youngster to draw a chicken; this isn't necessarily a negative thing, and, for some people, it's what they're looking for. Breeders are beginning to use more creative crossings that result in a larger range of colors for both eggs and plumage. Originally, hybrids were only crosses of the more productive laying pure species, such as the Rhode Island Red.

Due to their abundant egg production, hybrids can be quite active, which makes them slightly more hostile toward one another. As they vigorously scratch and forage, their habitat can suffer. However, for beginners or anyone looking for a steady supply of eggs, their natural hardiness, predictability, and lower cost make them a suitable option.

In addition to the previously mentioned Rhode Star and Goldline, popular hybrid breeds contain Columbian Blacktail, Nera, White Star, and Speckeldy. If a pure breed is what you're after, you'll probably start by weeding them out based on appearance before looking more closely at the traits to choose the one that best fits your needs. Keep in mind that some species, like Orpingtons, have the potential to grow enormous, but for people who have limited space, many pure breeds also offer bantam variations that are smaller replicas of the large breeds and necessitate much less space and less cramped accommodations.

3.2 How to choose the best chicken breeds for meat production?

Here are some useful hints for limiting your options and a few recommended breeds that adapt well to various surroundings.

- **Climate Tolerance**

Each chicken breed has a different climatic tolerance. Make sure to choose breeds appropriate for the country and region in which you plan to grow the animals.

Although most birds can acclimate to cold weather, many struggle in hotter areas. While lighter birds thrive in hotter temperatures, heavier birds typically thrive in colder regions of the country. Certain breeds thrive in both hot and cold regions.

- **Available space**

Choose birds based on the amount of room you have available for your flock. Breeds that are active do better on wide, spacious farmland. They struggle with confinement. However, several breeds of chicken have calm dispositions to cope with close confinement in urban or backyard environments.

- **Temperament**

Choose breeds with placid temperaments if you're just starting out in your chicken-raising endeavor or want your kids to engage with the animals. When rearing hens in constrained areas, in urban or suburban settings, or both, it is a good idea to select calm animals.

- **Egg production**

Make careful to select a breed of chicken that produces eggs of good to exceptional quality if you intend to raise hens exclusively for their eggs. A healthy hen will lay between 125 and 175 eggs annually. Very good production is between 150 and 200 eggs per hen per year. Excellent output reaches 230 eggs annually, and under the correct circumstances, some can produce as much as 300 eggs annually.

- **Egg size and color**

Egg size and color may seem like unimportant factors when choosing a chicken breed, but they can make a big difference. Some varieties, such as Easter Eggers, can lay eggs of various hues. In addition to egg size, egg yield is also affected by egg size. In general, smaller breeds lay smaller eggs; therefore, if you want bigger eggs, look for bigger, heavier types.

- **Maturation rate**

If you are growing chickens to make meat, you should look at how fast the birds you are interested in grow up. In order to increase meat production, meat breeds are typically designed for quick growth. When growing laying chickens, maturity rate is another significant factor to take into account. Breeds that grow faster than others and lay eggs early include.

Popular meat-producing breeds as examples:

- **Cornish cross**

When growing chickens for meat, Cornish Cross and related hybrids are very popular.

In just 6-8 weeks, they can gain enough weight to weigh 12 pounds. They are the most popular option among backyard breeders and commercial meat producers due to their great growth rate.

Furthermore, compared to dual-purpose chicken breeds, the Cornish Cross grows quicker and has better flavor. Additionally, it is preferred to breed that are raised solely for their meat. The Cornish Cross has relatively little activity due to its incredibly rapid rate of growth.

These chickens are ideal for the dinner table since they have broad breasts, big thighs, and legs, as well as enhanced golden skin.

- Size: Extra-large (5+ processed pounds)
- Taste: Typical for you
- Appearance: large, white breasts with a flawless pearlescent sheen.
- The rapid rate of growth!
- Egg Production: Very little (not advised for egg production)

- **Freedom rangers**

The goal when creating the Freedom Rangers was to produce good pasture-fed meat birds.

They were developed especially for the market for pesticide-free meat. These hens are more adept at locating food than Cornish Crosses and thrive on low-protein meals. They are, therefore, ideal hens for free-ranging in a big pen.

They can live off of maize feed and field grubs and still remain in excellent eating conditions. Although tints of golden and grey are also common, these chickens are typically red with many barred or speckled black feathers.

Despite the fact that Freedom Rangers take longer to raise, many people prefer their flavor to that of other breeds. They are perfect for rotisserie ovens, according to some.

- Largest size after the Cornish Cross. 5lbs+
- Flavor: Slightly sweeter
- Appearance: Variable skin tones, smaller breasts
- Growth is rapid!

- Recommendations against producing eggs
  o **Orpington**

Another large breed of chicken is the Orpington, which may reach up to 7-8 pounds on average for females.

Despite being excellent layers, they are primarily employed as broilers because of the tenderness and incredible flavor of their flesh. These birds have a large body and a short, curved back with a U-shaped underline.

- Large (8 to 10 pounds before processing)
- Whiteish skin color (also depending on variety)
- Taste: Slightly sweeter, more flavorful, and fatter (in a good manner) than other breeds
- Growth Rate: Slow (18-week process)
- Good egg production may produce 180 eggs a year.

3.3 Processing of chicken: timing of slaughter and preparation of flesh

First and foremost, it's critical to comprehend that chickens experience several developmental stages as they grow up. Most importantly, all hens mature at various speeds based on a variety of variables, such as breed, feeding regimens, and feed kinds.

Making the appropriate decisions when it comes to the slaughter of your chickens will be aided by your knowledge of the traits, rates of growth, and finishing sizes specific to your breed.

It often takes up to seven weeks for broiler chickens—chickens reared for eating—to reach market weight. Each chicken is hand-caught at the farm once it has attained the correct size and weight by personnel who have been trained in humane handling. Chickens are moved into modular bins or holding cages throughout this operation in order to prevent harm to the birds or to other birds while being transported to the processing facility and to allow air to circulate.

The subsequent procedures are broken down to provide a more thorough explanation of the remaining steps involved in killing and processing chickens for meat:

1. **Reaching the processing facility**

The well-being of hens is carefully monitored both throughout their brief journey to the processing factory and during their time being reared on the farm. The distance is usually less than 60 miles. Thus the birds don't travel far.

2. Stunning

Every effort is taken in contemporary poultry processing facilities to ensure that hens are processed promptly and painlessly. Prior to being slaughtered, they are first rendered comatose and pain-free.

The main technique used in the US to sedate broilers before slaughter is "electrical stunning." It is the main technique used to make birds unconscious. The United States has a small number of facilities that use broiler CAS (controlled atmosphere stunning) systems. These techniques use carbon dioxide to make birds unconscious. Another CAS system that is used to stun birds lowers atmospheric pressure.

Both systems must be monitored, adjusted, and managed effectively to guarantee they are upholding criteria for humane care while they are functioning well, making them both equally compassionate.

3. Slaughter

In order to reduce agony, technology makes slaughter exceedingly swift. An unconscious bird may usually be killed with just one cut to the throat, but if the blade happens to miss for whatever reason, skilled personnel are ready to immediately euthanize any remaining birds. A quick and humane slaughter procedure depends on maintaining the machinery and this backup "human" system.

4. "Evisceration"

Birds that have been killed go through a process to have their feathers removed. This is required to get the bird ready for processing. The chicken is first placed through a hot water bath, which is intended to help release feathers. The process of removing feathers is carried out by a device known as a "picker," which has a large number of tiny rubber "fingers" that rotate in order to do so.

The birds are then taken to an "eviscerating" line where the feet, or "paws," are removed along with the feathers.

Every component of the bird is utilized; for instance, in Asia, chicken feet are prized as a delicacy, and some animal feeds use rendered feathers as a source of protein.

5. Chilling and cleaning

The corpses are washed once the organs have been removed, and then they are examined.

As an extra step to reduce germs even more, each bird can be rinsed with an organic solution and water. The Food and Drug Administration, also known as the FDA, and the USDA both strictly regulate any drug used for this purpose and have given their approval for usage in food production.

According to research, using these rinses improves the overall wholesomeness of finished items rather than posing any health risks to people. The birds are again inspected for quality, food safety, and wholesomeness prior to this step, which involves cooling them to a lower temperature in order to maintain them fresh and clean. They adhere to strict regulatory and commercial criteria for each bird that enters the chilling process.

6. **USDA inspection**

Each bird is examined throughout the evisceration process by a worker from the processing facility and a USDA inspector. Each chicken is visually inspected by USDA inspectors who search for illnesses, feces, or bruising.

Any birds that have problems are flagged, condemned, and the problem is fixed. It's crucial to keep in mind that chickens are healthier than they have ever been and rejected parts make up under 1% of total production.

7. **Additional testing**

Following chilling, businesses and the USDA conduct microbiological tests on products and equipment at chicken plants to further guarantee food safety. Tests for germs like Salmonella are included in this.

These procedures are so effective that the percentage of products that test positive for Salmonella is negligible in comparison to the total output. The most recent USDA statistics show that 2.7% of whole birds tested positive for Salmonella in big operations, which is representative of most U.S. chicken production. This is significantly less than the USDA's 7.5 percent threshold.

Remind yourself that when handled properly and cooked to an average temperature of 165° Fahrenheit, all chicken is healthy to consume. Despite the industry's best efforts to eliminate pathogens before chicken products reach customers, it's still crucial that consumers follow these basic guidelines for cooking to avoid getting sick.

8. "Second Processing"

The carcass is usually sliced and deboned to suit a number of various products after being thoroughly tested and cooled. Chicken sold fresh or frozen to consumers, as well as chicken utilized in restaurants and exported, may be among these products. This includes convenience foods like thighs, drumsticks, wings, leg quarters, breasts, and more that are typically found in "tray-packs" at your neighborhood grocery stores.

Each piece of chicken is ultimately subjected to over 300 safety checks for quality, wholesomeness, and food safety before being distributed to consumers.

9. Packaging

After the chicken has been divided into pieces, trays have been packed with wrapped chicken. In order to make sure it meets or surpasses consumer and customer expectations, the wrapped product is then examined once more.

Products are chilled by passing them, in baskets, through a "blast tunnel." This is done to prolong the product's freshness and increase its shelf life. The product does not freeze despite being severely chilled during this process.

The product is weighed, its price is printed, and safe handling guidelines are attached to the package once it has been adequately refrigerated. Chicken package labels must first receive USDA approval before being applied to a product.

A last check with a metal detector is performed on the item to make sure nothing that shouldn't be there is within the package.

The goods are then finally put into boxes with a label applied to the outside. This label includes the date packaged, the USDA seal of approval, and the plant's establishment number so that the product may be linked back to the facility where it was made.

10. Shipping

The chicken is finally en route to the market near you. Trailers are checked to make sure they are operating properly, are adequately cooled, and are clean before the finished product is loaded onto trucks.

A tamper-evident seal is applied to the trailer when a cargo load is finished. In order to guarantee product safety and wholesomeness, the seal is not broken until the consumer receives the product.

Retail goods are typically distributed to a retailer's warehouse the day following their departure from the manufacturing facility. The day after delivery is typically when chicken goods are added to corporate grocery stores.

3.4 How to keep raw chicken fresh?

Typically, fresh chicken is kept in the fridge for later use. The freshness and nutritional worth will be lost if you don't know how to store it, though. Therefore, please see the preservation technique below.

- **Refrigerator: how long?**

The refrigerator is the most typical place to store raw chicken, although the storage time will vary based on whether the chicken is kept in the refrigerator or freezer. The following are the recommended times to store fresh poultry meat in the refrigerator, namely chicken, per the (USDA) United States Department of Agriculture:

Cooling compartment: 1-2 days (0 to 5 degrees Celsius). Up to nine months in a freezer. But be sure to store the meat properly at a secure temperature.

- **Refrigerating raw chicken?**

Raw chicken should be stored properly to maintain its nutritional content and flavor while reducing the risk of food poisoning from rotting, rancid flesh. Here are the steps you should take to refrigerate raw chicken:

1. Wrap the meat tightly. In order to prevent contamination, it is essential to wash the chicken and place it in a sealed container before covering the meat and keeping it in the refrigerator. A hybrid of raw foods. The chicken can be wrapped in numerous layers to avoid freezing, which would alter its flavor, color, and dehydration. Consequently, it will lose its flavor after processing.

2. Maintain a consistent temperature in the refrigerator by placing neatly wrapped fresh chicken meat inside. It is required to regulate and guarantee that the temperature is kept at -25 degrees Celsius while stored in the freezer. Check the temperature carefully to avoid affecting the preserved meat's quality.

3. Organize the refrigerator. The refrigerator's layout is crucial for preserving the temp. of fresh chicken. To split food and conserve space in the refrigerator, avoid packing the refrigerator with too much food.

4. Be mindful of the expiration date; raw chicken can last up to 9 months in the freezer, but it loses much of its flavor after that. Use it up within a month for optimal results. Delicious and wholesome, yet fresh. In order to determine which cuts of meat should be consumed first and which can be stored for longer, it is important to keep track of when they were stored.

- **Raw chicken storage without refrigeration?**

In the event of a power outage or lack of a refrigerator, raw chicken can be stored outside by cleaning and then drying it. Then, to keep out dust and insects, keep the chicken in a cool, dry area with a table cage or mosquito net.

Salt or other seasonings can be added to chicken to get rid of the smell. Pre-processing chicken by frying, frying, microwaving, and then storing it in a dry place is another way to extend its shelf life.

- **Ideally, defrost raw chicken**

When removing fresh chicken from the freezer compartment for use, it must also be fully defrosted to preserve the meat's flavor and nutritional content. You can use a variety of methods to thaw food, such as:

Defrost meat in the microwave by placing it in a microwave-safe dish (such as a glass bowl or plastic container) and selecting the recipe. Defrosting level. While this method is quick, the meat frequently loses flavor and some of its nutritional value.

In order to defrost the chicken using water, place it in a ziplock bag and then into a bucket of cold water. Although it takes a while, this method results in meat that is still tasty and nutritious. In order to reduce defrosting time, hot water should be avoided, as it increases the possibility of bacterial growth.

The best way to thaw meat kept in the freezer is to remove the chicken from the freezer and place it in a larger dish or box to catch the melting ice as it drips off the meat. Other foods kept in the refrigerator won't be affected by it. While this process is time-consuming, the meat's flavor and nutritional value are virtually guaranteed.

Chapter 4: Nutrition

We keep chickens because they are an efficient source of eggs and meat from other feedstuffs like cereal grains. It's crucial that our chickens eat well. Feed is used by chickens for two main reasons:

- as a source of energy to sustain bodily functions such as maintaining body temperature, eating, walking, and digesting feed,
- to serve as a foundation for the growth of bone, flesh, feathers, and eggs.

4.1 Why do hens need a well-balanced diet?

To keep your chickens content and healthy, you must provide them with a balanced and nutritious diet. Since they are omnivores, layer hens can eat a wide range of different foods.

To ensure that your hens receive all the nutrients they require, you should feed them primarily commercial poultry feed of high quality. These feeds are composed of a blend of grit (ground limestone or oyster shell), grains (corn, soybeans, and oats), and vitamins (calcium) and can be found in pellet, mash, or crumbed forms. Other seeds and grains (like wheat and corn) could also be dispersed in the surroundings to complement their diet and stimulate natural foraging behavior. The feed can be delivered in a feed container or dispenser.

A range of fresh fruits and vegetables can be provided every day in addition to high-quality chicken feed. Fruit and vegetable peels, bananas, apples, spinach, berries, bok choy, carrots, cabbage, silver beet, or broccoli are a few examples of vegetables and fruits that are raw that can be fed. Your hens may also receive a tiny bit of cooked food as a treat, such as pasta, rice, bread, or beans.

Depending on your hens' age, breed, size, and egg-laying status, their nutritional needs will vary and change. If the eggs from your chickens have fragile or thin shells, your birds may be lacking in calcium, necessitating the use of a calcium supplement. Ask a veterinarian, an established poultry owner, the neighborhood poultry association, or the local poultry fancier's society for feeding advice to make sure your hens are receiving the right amount and kind of food.

Never feed hens food scraps that are rotten or spoiled or that are heavy in fat, salt, or other unhealthy ingredients. In particular, raw potatoes, avocados, garlic, chocolate, onions, uncooked rice, citrus fruits, and uncooked beans should not be offered to hens. It is important to consult an expert before deciding whether to feed a particular food type to your chickens if you are doubtful of its safety.

In the absence of access to dirt or grass, providing your chickens with a steady supply of grit like ground-up shells, stones, or gravel will go a long way toward easing their digestion. Make sure none of the garden plants, including removed weeds, that hens have access to are hazardous to chickens. For free-range hens, weed grass is preferred over a monoculture lawn.

Of course, clean water needs to be accessible at all times, and during the colder months, ensure sure any ice blocking the way is cleared every morning. The optimal placement of water containers keeps chickens from bending over to reach them.

Something may be wrong if your chickens' feeding habits change or if they suddenly lose their appetite. If your bird's feeding behavior or appetite changes, you should visit a veterinarian.

4.2 Chicken feed types

For the majority of the thousands of years that humans have kept chickens, their lifestyle has been more like that of a stray cat than that of the modern chicken. They typically foraged freely and consumed insects and different vegetation. Some may have had access to kitchen scraps or a compost heap containing garbage and worms.

The majority of backyard chickens today are confined, so they are unable to walk into the yard of a neighbor. It doesn't require long for these animals to consume all of the grass, and before you realize it, they're only consuming grain feed.

After World War II, when chickens were raised on industrial farms, they began to eat primarily grain-based feed. Since those early days, a lot has been learned about the nutritional requirements of developing birds and a wide range of feeds have been developed for a number of purposes. The description of typical breeds and feed, along with their applications, are given below.

- **Chick starter**

In order to satisfy the dietary needs of young chicks, feed for the starter is a protein-rich variant of chicken feed. A diet of water and starting feed is usually sufficient for newborn chicks to survive for the first 6 weeks of their lives. The starter feed must be phased out once the chicks reach the age of six weeks since the starter feed's high protein content, which ranges from 20 to 24 percent, aids in the development of young chicks into active pullets. Otherwise, the starter feed's excess protein can harm the liver.

Starting/grower feed, which is simply a sort of feed that hens can take from one to twenty weeks of age, is a variety of feed that can be used to further complicate issues. But if there are any questions, read the label and find the nearest poultry expert.

- **Grower feed**

In many aspects, grower feed is similar to hen feed for young chickens. A chicken between the ages of six and twenty weeks has considerably different nutritional needs than a young chick. In essence, grower feed has a protein concentration of 16–18% but less calcium than standard layer feed. In a nutshell, grower feed encourages your teenage chookies' continued growth without overdosing them with nutrients better suited for laying hens that are fully matured. Your hens will be prepared for layer feed once they start laying eggs, so watch for that.

- **Layer feed**

The majority of your flock's food will be delicious layer feed for the majority of their lifespan. The clever protein, calcium, and other vitamin and mineral ratio in layer feed promotes your flock to produce superior eggs. Similar to grower feed in terms of protein content, layer feed has between 16 and 18%. The eggshells are crisp, clear, and crunchy because of the additional calcium in it. However, feeding young pullets or baby chicks layer feed won't satisfy their special dietary needs. Only chickens that are around 20 weeks old or have begun to lay eggs should be given layer feed.

- **Mash**

Simply defined, the mash is an uncooked, loose kind of poultry feed. Mash is the best type of chicken feed available. It has a feel like potting soil. Mash is typically offered to baby chicks since it is simple to digest, but it is also sometimes given to fully-grown chickens. Some hen keepers make a porridge-like treat by mixing mash and hot water, which the chickens will love. However, keep in mind that using this technique might result in the feed expiring more quickly. Keep in mind that the major drawback of chicken feed products with a mashed texture is that this texture frequently leads to an increase in accidental waste.

- **Crumble**

Simply put, crumble is a rough form of mash that produces less compact pellets. Crumble is a kind of semi-loose chicken feed that resembles oatmeal in texture and is a little bit simpler to handle than mash. For their flock, some chicken enthusiasts use crumble as a transitional food between mash and pellets. Others assert that their female hens simply like the crumbly texture better. Whatever your motivations for choosing to crumble over mash or pellets, the health of your flock shouldn't be much affected by your decision.

- **Pellets**

The most popular type of chicken feed is probably pellets. Pellets are essentially tiny, compact cylinders of delicious chicken feed, just as the name implies. Pellets have the advantage of maintaining their shape, so if your females unintentionally tip their feeder over, nothing will be lost. Pellets are frequently the initial option for the majority of backyard chicken keepers because they are simple to manage, store, and serve.

- **Shell grit**

Some novice poultry keepers don't realize how crucial shell grit is to the diet of their flock. In essence, shell grit has two main uses. For starters, shell grit is high in calcium, which helps your ladies produce tasty eggs with robust and thick shells. Insufficient shell grit in a chicken's diet can lead to abnormal egg development, leading to the production of eggs that might put off even the most ardent fan of the chicken's eggcellent gift. Second, hens' gizzards accumulate shell grit, which helps them pulverize their grain and more easily digest their meals. Shell grit is an essential part of the diet for all adult chickens and should be provided to them in a dish separate from their laying feed. Don't worry too much about serving quantities because chickens can control their calcium intake; most girls can recognize when they've had enough.

- **Chicken scratch**

Chicken feed is different from chicken scratch. Consider poultry scratch as a snack for your flock. Although chickens love to eat broken corn and other grains, the majority of chicken scratch kinds are not very good for their waistlines. Your flock will benefit greatly from chicken scratch as a source of energy, and it will also keep them warm in the winter when the weather gets chilly. Chicken scratch is a tasty treat that every chicken deserves occasionally, but it shouldn't be seen as a replacement for a balanced diet.

- **Medication vs. no medication**

Starter and grower chickens kinds frequently eat medicated chicken feed since it is a simple approach to protect your flock from coccidiosis and other poultry diseases. Simply said, the medicated feed contains amprolium, a substance that aids in defending your daughters against potentially fatal and serious diseases that they may contract as young children. Therefore, if your chickens have been vaccinated, do not serve them medicated feed, as the amprolium's effects are incompatible with the vaccine.

- **Fermented feed**

It's simple to increase the enzyme and vitamin content of your chicken feed, make it simpler for your chickens to digest, and remove toxins by fermenting it. Because fermented feed is so dense, it also gives your chickens a longer-lasting feeling of fullness. As a result, your chickens will produce fewer droppings each week, and your weekly chicken feed expenses will decline. - EGGCELLENT!

- **Broiler varieties**

For those raising chickens for consumption, there are broiler feed options available. There are three main varieties: starter, grower, and finisher, without getting too hung up on the minutiae. In essence, broiler chicken feed has a denser protein content, which helps the flock to develop larger and more quickly. Broiler chicken feed is absolutely not recommended for laying hens because the increased protein may not always be good for the health of your flock.

4.3 Useful dietary additions for hens

The vitamins listed below can help your flock have contented, healthy chickens.

- **Protein**

Chickens need more protein in their diets throughout the winter or the molting season. Scrambled eggs or mealworms are excellent additions.

What to eat: 2-3 times a week, one scrambled egg is served per chicken. 2-3 times a week, 1 tablespoon of mealworms per fowl. (These protein additives can't actually be consumed in excess)

- **Grit**

Non-free-range or confined chickens without access to soil or gravel must consume grit. Chickens will pick up tiny gravel fragments in the wild and store them in their gizzards. These little bits of gravel serve as the chickens' teeth, breaking down their meal into smaller pieces.

How to feed: In a separate bowl from their food, grit can be given to them at their discretion.

- **Calcium**

Calcium is necessary for the normal development of eggshells. There should be enough calcium in the majority of layer foods to satisfy your hens. Calcium is crucial because, without enough of it, hens will begin to draw calcium from their bones to make eggshells. It's time to give a calcium supplement if you observe soft-shell eggs, which are eggs with a rubbery shell as opposed to a hard one. The majority of feed retailers that sell chicken goods also include an oyster shell supplement, or you can feed your hens dried, crushed eggshells.

What to eat: Free-choice calcium can be provided alongside food in a separate container.

- **Apple cider vinegar**

There are numerous health benefits associated with apple cider vinegar. If your chickens have respiratory problems, it thins their mucous. Furthermore, it can alkalize the body, which makes internal parasites uncomfortable while assisting with digestion.

Different types of apple cider vinegar exist. The type with the "Mother" still present is the healthiest. Most of the advantages to health come from the mother, which is the living bacteria in the vinegar. The Braggs brand is a wise choice.

What to eat: To one gallon of fresh water, add one tablespoon of ACV. This should be alternated every few days with regular water.

- **Probiotics**

Probiotics support the immunological and digestive systems of your chicken. You can sprinkle them on the meal for your flock or add them to the water for drinking.

How to provide food: Probiotics powders can be found at the majority of feed retailers. For instructions, read the package labels.

- **Garlic**

A fantastic remedy for illness is garlic. Especially the potential onset of respiratory conditions throughout the winter.

How to feed: You may either use powdered garlic or chopped, fresh garlic that has been ground up and added to the feed per gallon of feed, 1 tablespoon.

4.4 How to make homemade chicken feed?

Making your own poultry feed allows you to save money and know what your chickens are consuming. These recipes call for organic ingredients if you wish to feed your poultry organically. Make the laying hen feed or the broiler feed, depending on what kind of chickens you intend to raise. Both dishes are nutrient- and protein-rich, which will help your chickens get the nutrition they need.

- **Making laying hens' chicken feed**

Ingredients

- 19 kilograms (41 pounds) of soy
- 49 kilograms (7 pounds) of whole maize meal
- 14 kilograms (31 pounds) of maize bran
- 13 kilograms (28 pounds) of fish meal
- 5.9 kilograms (13 pounds) of limestone powder

Directions

- Count the ingredients and put them in a jar. Whole maize meal weighing 49 kg (107 pounds), soya weighing 19 kg (41 pounds), fish meal weighing 13 kg (28 pounds), maize bran weighing 14 kg (31 pounds), and limestone powder weighing 5.9 kg (13 pounds) should all be combined in a container. To mix and store the 100 kg (220 pounds) of chicken feed that this recipe yields, you will need a sizable bucket or barrel.
- The ingredients should be completely blended after being mixed. To

- properly distribute all the components throughout the container, stir the feed using a shovel. This makes sure that the chickens get all the nutrients they need from the food they eat.
- Each chicken should receive 0.13 kg (0.28 pounds) of food each day. Divide the amount of food required by the number of chickens you have. For instance, 0.76 kg (1.68 pounds) of grain would be needed for 6 hens multiplied by 0.13 kg (0.28 pounds). Spread the food out on the ground or put it in a feeder to attract the birds.
- The chicken feed can be kept for up to six months in a cool, dry location. The best places to store poultry feed are garages or barns. Before feeding the hens, inspect the grain for rodents, pests, and mold. It is best to discard tainted feed if possible.
- **Preparing broiler feed**

  Ingredients
  - 110 kilograms (250 pounds) of broken corn
  - 11 kilograms (25 pounds) of rolled oats
  - 68 kilograms (150 pounds) of ground, roasted soybeans
  - 4.5 kilograms (10 pounds) of aragonite, or calcium powder
  - 11 kilograms (25 pounds) of alfalfa meal
  - 11 kilograms (25 pounds) of bone meal or fish
  - 6.8 kilograms (15 pounds) of nutritionally balanced poultry

  Directions
  - In a container, combine the broken corn and the ground-roasted soybeans. In a sizable container, like a feed or barrel container, add 68 kg (150 pounds) of crushed roasted soybeans and 110kg (250 pounds) of cracked corn. With a shovel, combine the ingredients until they are well combined.
  - The combination should be combined with the alfalfa meal, rolled oats, and bone or fish meal. Rolling oats, alfalfa meal, and fish or bone meal, each weighing 11 kg (25 pounds), should be added to the container. Until everything is dispersed equally throughout the container, combine the ingredients with the soybeans and cracked corn.

- Add the poultry Nutri-balancer and aragonite to the container. Add 15 pounds (6.8 kg) of poultry Nutri-balancer and 4.5 kg (10 pounds) of calcium powder (aragonite) to the feed. The powders must be evenly distributed throughout the meal, therefore thoroughly combine the components. The addition of the poultry Nutri-balancer to the feed is crucial since it guarantees the hens get all the nutrients they need for rapid development.

- Feed the mixture to each chicken daily at a rate of 0.27 kg (0.6 pounds). Determine the total amount of feed needed by multiplying the number of chickens by the feed per chicken. Feed the animals once daily by placing the food in a feeder or by dumping it on the ground.

- For a maximum of six months, keep the chicken feed covered in a container. Put a lid on the feed container and keep it somewhere cool and dry, such as in a barn or garage. This will lessen the risk of the feed becoming contaminated or growing mold.

4.5 How to stop wasting food

Chickens are notoriously sloppy eaters. The habit of a chicken scratching the ground in search of food is one of the instincts for survival. They will attempt to scratch at grain even if it is neatly hung in a feeding container, scattering it widely and wasting a good deal of it.

Here are some suggestions to reduce food waste.

- Do not combine treats and chicken feed.
- Feed the chickens in rations.
- Organize your dinner every night.
- Raise the chicken feed.
- Modify the chicken feed you use.
- The hen feed should be fermented

4.6 Calculating chickens' food consumption

Due to the fact that every breed and flock is unique, determining the optimal quantity of daily chicken feed will require time and observation. There is, however, a basic figure that will give you a good starting point: 1/4 pound per fully developed chicken per day. This means that in a week, each chicken will consume about 1.5 pounds of feed.

This sum will change depending on the size and age of your birds. The best approach to determine your flock's needs is to inspect the feeders after they've eaten their fill. Simply take note of any remaining feed and change the amount the following day. As a general rule, it is preferable to provide excess feed rather than insufficient, as wasted food is preferable to poultry that is malnourished.

A laying chicken will consume roughly 1.75 pounds of feed each week as an adult. This equates to approximately 3.5–4 ounces (about 1/4 lb) (or nearly 1/2 cup) of feed per bird per day).

For the first eight weeks of their lives, baby chicks consume about an ounce or two of feed per day. This equals 3/4 to 1 pound of feed every week. And they'll consume three times as much liquid as they do food.

How to manage kitchen trash and leftover food

Providing chickens with table scraps increases the variety of their diet and is a wonderful way to dispose of leftovers. Blueberries, watermelon, and leftover strawberries are chicken favorites. The berries are loaded with antioxidants, making them quite healthful.

Tips for feeding chickens leftovers

- Always consider your flock's health when serving leftovers. If you feed them junk food, their health will suffer. Ensure that the scraps you offer them are wholesome and still quite fresh. Never give them anything moldy.

- To prevent vermin and other creatures out of the coop, just feed your hens what they can consume in a single day. Any leftovers should be taken out once the birds have gone to bed in the evening. Any remaining food will draw predators like raccoons, skunks, foxes, and mice in addition to rats and mice.

- Keep in mind that feeding animals things like blueberries will turn their feces a dark bluish color. Do not be alarmed; once they have digested the berries, this will disappear.

- Your hen will typically consume about a quarter-pound of food per day, and table leftovers should not account for more than ten percent of her daily diet. Of course, you won't measure it precisely; you'll just have to guess, and sometimes they'll get more and other times less.

- o You should only feed scraps in the late afternoon or evening to ensure that your chickens finish their feed first. Rather than simply tossing the foodstuff on the ground, use a containeror bowl.

For chickens to be healthy and productive, appropriate and safe food must be provided. For healthy, abundant egg production, hens need a balanced diet that fits their nutritional needs. Giving them harmful or inappropriate food can cause major health issues, decreased productivity, and even death.

Chapter 5: The chicken coop

A chicken coop or hen house is a structure where chickens or other fowl are kept safe and secure. There may be nest boxes and perches in the house.

If you want to maintain hens, you'll need to build them a nice coop and keep them safe from predators. Consider that predators can leap into, burrow under, and gnaw on any hen house if given the opportunity.

5.1 How to locate a hen house?

For your chickens' health, safety, and general welfare, it's crucial to pick a place for a hen house or chicken coop. When choosing a place for your hen house, keep the following things in mind:

- **Space:** Make sure you have enough room for the amount of your flock. Chickens require space to roost, wander around, and lay eggs. Hens should have as much room as possible in their coops. Each hen will require a different amount of space, depending on their breed, size, age, hen house type, and external environmental factors (such as temperature and humidity). 2-3.5 m2 of usable floor space per hen is the bare minimum that should be provided by a hen house; however, hens should ideally be provided with more space.

- **Protection against predators:** Pick a place that is protected from potential predators like foxes, raccoons, and raptors. Avoid locations with tall grass or dense bushes since they could be used as cover by predators. To safeguard your chickens, think about erecting fencing or other barriers.

- **Ventilation:** In order to keep moisture, ammonia, and aromas from building up in the hen coop, proper ventilation is crucial. To keep the air clean and avoid respiratory problems in your chickens, pick a place that allows for good airflow. Avoid low-lying locations that could get wet or flood easily.

- **Sunlight:** Chickens require direct sunshine to be healthy and lay eggs. Pick a spot that receives plenty of sunlight all day. The hen's house is kept dry and helps regulate moisture with the help of sunlight.

- **Drainage:** To avoid floods and waterlogging during rainy seasons, choose a location that has good drainage. Avoid regions where there is a lot of standing water because it could harm your chickens' health.

- **Food and water availability:** Think about your convenience while picking a spot to keep your chickens fed and watered. For convenience in watering your flock, think about its accessibility to a water supply.

- **Convenience:** Think about how the location will affect your everyday activities and hen house management. Pick a spot that is convenient for cleaning, collecting eggs, and other routine tasks.

- **Laws and zoning regulations:** Make sure to abide by local zoning regulations and any applicable laws when keeping chickens. Find out if raising chickens or constructing hen houses is prohibited where you live, and then pick a spot that complies.

5.2 Materials required for construction

Whether you call it a chicken coop, chicken house, or hen house, the supplies you'll need to build one depend on its layout, size, and purpose. However, the following is a broad list of supplies that might be required:

1. **Supporting structure**
    - The henhouse's framework is made of wood, iron, or PVC pipes.
    - Fasteners for securing the structural elements together, such as brackets, screws, and bolts.
    - If necessary, use concrete or gravel to lay the foundation.

2. **Roof and walls**
    - The walls and roof of the hen house should be constructed out of plywood, wood planks, or metal sheets.
    - For ventilation openings or windows, use netting or wire mesh.
    - Depending on the environment, insulation material for the walls and roof (such as fiberglass or foam board)

3. **Flooring**
    - Depending on your preferences and financial constraints, the hen house's flooring could be made of gravel, rammed earth, or concrete.
    - Bedding materials to make the hens' habitat more cozy, such as wood shavings or straw.

4. **Systems for Locking and Opening:**
   - Metal, PVC, or wooden doors must be used for the main entrance and any other access points.
   - Windows with netting or wire mesh for ventilation and light.
   - Vents or flaps for controlling the temperature and ventilation inside the coop.

5. **Miscellaneous**
   - Construction equipment, including screwdrivers, hammers, saws, and measuring tapes.
   - Protective equipment for safety during building, such as gloves, masks, and goggles.
   - The wood surfaces should be finished with paint or stain to prevent deterioration.

5.3 The best hen house size and design

There is no one "perfect" chicken coop layout for a backyard flock, but there are several elements to look at and take into account when making your decision, whether you decide to construct your own coop, turning a garden shed or children's playhouse into a coop, or buying a pre-made structure.

A decent chicken coop should have certain characteristics in addition to being functional and secure in order to protect your chicks from predators and maintain their health.

- **Size**

Depending on the breeds you intend to raise, each hen will need 3-4 square feet of indoor floor area. Greater breeds like Jersey Giants or Brahmas require more space than bantams, which require less. Think about how many chickens you intend to raise in the long run, because it's far simpler to go big at the outset (whether you're building or buying) than it is to try to expand. The best kind of chickens for your backyard are described in further detail.

- **Elevation**

In contrast to coops placed directly on the ground, raised coops are more safe (unless you place your chicken coop on concrete), as this will stop predators from digging underneath the coop to try to get inside and prevent a wooden floor from decaying. A elevated coop will protect your chickens from the hot summer sun and the cold winter rain and snow. The chickens can fit underneath the coop with ease if it is raised up at least 8-12 inches upon cement blocks or wooden legs. Chickens that are allowed to roam freely can protect themselves from birds of prey by roosting on an elevated coop.

- **Flooring**

The floor of a coop should be made of cement or concrete for the highest level of safety, but this material can be quite pricey. Predators may easily breach dirt floors. The most prevalent flooring type is wood. Inexpensive vinyl flooring can be used to cover a wooden floor, making cleanup simple and preventing poultry mites from penetrating the surface.

- **Roosts**

Per hen, allow 8" of roosting bar as a general rule. Using 2/4 with the 4-inch side pointing up works well since chickens like to sleep flat-footed rather than clutching a bar like wild birds. In the winter, the flat side assists in keeping the hens' feet warm and free of frostbite.

- **Nesting boxes**

If you have more than three or four laying hens, you should provide one nesting box, but don't be shocked if they all use the same box. Boxes should be 12-14 inches square, made of wood, plastic, or metal, and placed lower than your roosts to discourage resting in them, which can result in contaminated eggs. Wine barrels, timber crates, or plastic totes can all be recycled and repurposed as nests. You can also purchase commercial boxes to install in a homemade coop or repurposed shed. Whatever material you use, make sure to fill the nesting boxes with cozy bedding. Both straw and pine shavings work wonderfully. Curtains are not required.

- **Ventilation**

A chicken coop needs to have good ventilation all year round, and to avoid drafts when the chickens are sleeping, the vents should be placed higher than the chickens' heads. To keep predators away, all windows and vents must be covered with 1/4" or 1/2" hardware cloth. A decent guideline is to have windows or vents on 1/5 of your coop's total wall area.

- **Latches**

Secure latches are required for nesting box lids and coop doors. For greater predator-proofing, a spring-loaded eye hook or a latch with a carabiner is preferable. Raccoons can crank knobs, lift latches, and move deadbolts.

- **Location**

Location is crucial if your coop will be stationary as opposed to a mobile tractor-style coop. In hot climates, you should position your chicken enclosure in the shade. It is preferable to face your coop southward if you reside in a northern climate. Consider the distance between your chicken coop and your home as well as a water source.

Taking these things into account will help you pick a coop that will serve your needs (and those of your chickens) for many years to come.

Chapter 6: Chickens' health

While the idea of chickens getting sick can be frightening, the majority of the time, these issues can be handled at home. Taking care of an animal or bird in good health and in bad is a responsibility that comes with pet ownership. This involves making decisions about its food, shelter, and well-being, as well as knowing when it is unwell and providing it with the necessary treatment to recover from the sickness or choosing to put a suffering bird to death.

6.1 A sick hen's Signs and Intervention

Here are some of the most common signs that a hen is sick, as well as what you can do to help:

- **Gastrointestinal symptoms**

If your hen has diarrhea or other stomach problems, like throwing up or not going to the bathroom, it could be a sign of a bigger health problem. Keep an eye on your hen's behavior and observe the color and consistency of her droppings. It is best to visit a veterinarian for an accurate diagnosis and treatment if the symptoms continue or get worse.

To counteract dehydration, give your hen access to clean water. Don't give them any meals like rotten or moldy food that can make their digestive troubles worse. To prevent any potential diseases from spreading to the other hens in the flock, think about isolating the sick hen.

- **Decreased appetite and shaggy plumage**

Smooth, spotless feathers are a sign of a healthy hen. A health problem may be present if you observe that your hen's feathers are scruffy, dull, or unclean, and they are acting lethargic or with a diminished appetite.

Check your hen for any indications of external parasites like lice or mites, which could contribute to poor feather health. Maintain a clean, well-ventilated coop and nesting sites. Provide your hen with clean water and nutritious food to get the best results. Consult a vet for additional testing and treatment if the symptoms don't go away.

- **Difficulty breathing and coughing**

Smooth, spotless feathers are a sign of a healthy hen. A health problem may be present if you observe that your hen's feathers are scruffy, dull, or unclean, and they are acting lethargic or with a diminished appetite.

Check your hen for any indications of external parasites like lice or mites, which could contribute to poor feather health. Maintain a clean, well-ventilated coop and nesting sites. Provide your hen with clean water and nutritious food to get the best results. Consult a vet for additional testing and treatment if the symptoms don't go away.

- **Parasites and skin lesions**

Hens can develop skin sores and become infested with mites, lice, and other external parasites. These may itch the skin, cause feather loss, and be uncomfortable.

Check the skin of your hen frequently for any indications of blemishes, wounds, or apparent parasites. Immediately apply the proper poultry-safe medications to any infestations, as advised by a veterinarian. To stop the spread of parasites, keep the coop and the nesting places dry and clean.

How to handle illness and when to call a vet?

It's critical to intervene quickly if your hen exhibits any symptoms of disease. If the signs are minor, you can give the hen supportive care, such keeping her warm, giving her clean food and water, and separating her from the flock to stop the transmission of any potential diseases.

In extreme cases or if the symptoms persist or worsen despite your best efforts to treat them, you should seek the advice of a veterinarian with expertise in poultry health. Your hen can be nursed back to health with the assistance of a veterinarian's expert guidance, diagnostic testing, and prescription of the appropriate medications.

6.2 Preventing common diseases

Better-quality eggs are produced by healthy hens. They live longer as well. A healthy chicken can handle environmental pressures better. Additionally, they have a built-in advantage over common diseases and parasites. The secret to maintaining healthy backyard hens is proper coop management. Additionally, keeping the coop clean helps keep the chicken coop healthy. Here are some tips for keeping chickens healthy.

- **Ensure the poultry coop is tidy**

If you want to keep your birds in a healthy environment, you must regularly clean and disinfect the poultry house, its furnishings, and its equipment. Regularly remove trash, spilled feed, and other waste to stop the growth of infections. Use the disinfectants that are advised for your particular scenario and apply them in accordance with the manufacturer's instructions.

- **Regular check-ups and vaccinations**

One of the best methods for preventing infections in both people and animals is vaccination. For your animals, whether they are poultry, pets, or livestock, adhere to the appropriate immunization regimen. Taking your pet to the vet for regular checkups can help find any health problems early and stop them from getting worse.

- **Quarantine new animals**

New animals should be isolated from the rest of the herd for some time in a quarantine pen before being released into the wild. By putting new animals in quarantine, you may stop the spread of any diseases they might have and have time to watch them for any symptoms of disease before they interact with your healthy animals.

- **Keeping sick animals apart**

Chickens catch illnesses quickly. It's crucial to keep a close eye on your flock and get rid of any sick birds as soon as they appear. This helps shield others from illness. Additionally, eliminating sick chickens increases their chances of healing and prevents other neighboring birds from bullying them.

Make sure the bird is warm and well-hydrated after being segregated. If it isn't drinking or eating, offer it water that has been infused with the electrolyte solution, for example, AviLYTE, with a spoon or dropper till it is well-sufficient to drink by its own.

The flock should typically be treated if one of the birds in your flock has an infectious illness. Once one bird starts showing symptoms, it's likely that the rest of the flock has already been contaminated and will start showing symptoms as well. This is especially true for intestinal parasites like worms.

6.3 Poultry house cleanliness is crucial

Cleanliness and good hygiene are very important for keeping a poultry house healthy and effective. In order to avoid disease, ensure the welfare of the flock of hens, and ultimately improve the quality of chicken products, proper sanitation techniques are essential.

It is impossible to overestimate the importance of cleanliness in preventing sickness. A variety of pathogens, such as bacteria, viruses, and parasites, can thrive in poultry houses and cause illnesses like coccidiosis, Newcastle disease, avian influenza, and many others. Cleaning and disinfecting the chicken coop and its parts on a regular basis is important for preventing disease and keeping the flock healthy.

It takes several crucial actions to adequately clean the chicken coop and its accessories. To make cleaning easier, first take out all the equipment and poultry from the home. Dust, dirt, and cobwebs should be swept or otherwise removed from the floors, walls, and ceilings. With a water and mild detergent mixture, clean all surfaces, including the walls, floors, and equipment, paying special attention to any areas where dirt and waste have accumulated. Before reintroducing the chickens, properly rinse the house with clean water to get rid of all soap residue. Then, let the house completely dry out.

It's essential to manage manure and garbage properly in the chicken house to keep it clean. Accumulated manure can foster the development of pathogenic organisms and release poisonous gases like hydrogen sulfide and ammonia, which may be detrimental to the flock's health. It is possible to reduce the accumulation of germs and boost general hygiene in the chicken house by routinely removing manure and disposing of it properly or using it as fertilizer.

Additionally crucial to hen care is maintaining good personal hygiene. Chicken handlers should always use soap and water to clean their hands before and after working with chickens or chicken equipment. Personal protective equipment, like coveralls, gloves, or boots should be used to minimize disease transmission between regions of the farm as well as from one flock to another.

Chapter 7: : Self-sustenance

Some choices must be made when raising chickens, such as whether to focus on egg production or meat production. Some factors still need to be taken into account, despite claims that this choice is entirely based on personal preference. Depending on our specific demands, it may be more effective to raise certain breeds of chicken than others for egg or meat production.

7.1 Food preparation with hen's meat and eggs?

Millions of people need chicken meat and eggs, which are the richest sources of high-quality protein. Chicken meat is considered to be healthful, despite the fact that not all meat is, and it is typically less expensive than other meats. It is dependably of the highest quality, contains little saturated fat, can be supplemented with some necessary nutrients, and is in high demand all over the world.

Poultry meats are distinguished by having a balanced nutritional composition. These meats can be optimally absorbed into the diet at all ages thanks to their high vitamin, protein, and mineral content in combination with low-fat content (most of which is constituted of unsaturated fatty acids).

Eggs include several important nutrients, including the minerals zinc, copper, iodine, calcium, manganese, magnesium, sodium, potassium, chloride, and sulfur, in addition to the protein and fat that we need. The edible portion of the egg contains all these minerals as highly accessible organic chelates.

Quick facts about eggs:

- The best protein sources currently accessible are thought to be eggs.
- Fat makes up about 9% of an egg's weight and is almost always present in the yolk.
- The presence of cholesterol in eggs is well recognized.
- They are among the animal products that are most frequently consumed worldwide.

An adaptable food, eggs can be made in a variety of ways, including hard boiling, frying, scrambling, poaching, and baking. This makes including eggs in a diet quite straightforward.

Here are some recipes that use eggs as a main ingredient. These vary in terms of which are generally healthier:

- huevos rancheros
- kedgeree

- omelet
- pancakes
- quiche

Hard-boiled eggs are a popular snack, but eggs may also be used as a main dish in dishes like deviled eggs, which are great for parties and picnics. As a result, eggs are very adaptive to various lifestyles.

7.2 Recipes using eggs and chicken meat

The following recipes call for hen meat and eggs.

1. **<u>Traditional omelet with greens</u>**
   - Preparation time: 5 minutes
   - Cooking time: 15 minutes
   - Serving: 4

Ingredients
- 8 large-size eggs
- 3 tablespoons olive oil, divided
- 2 tablespoons butter, unsalted
- 2 tablespoons lemon juice
- 1 (yellow) onion, finely chopped
- 1 ounce Parmesan, finely grated
- 3 ounces of baby spinach
- Kosher salt

Directions
- In a large nonstick skillet, heat 1 tablespoon of oil over medium heat. Add the onion and cook for about 6 minutes or until soft. Place in a compact bowl.
- Whisk eggs, 1 tablespoon water, and 1/2 teaspoon salt in a sizable bowl. Butter is added once the skillet is brought back to medium. Eggs should be added and cooked while being regularly stirred with a rubber spatula until halfway set.
- Turn down the heat to low, cover the pan tightly, and cook the eggs for 4 to 5 minutes or until just set. Fold in half after adding sautéed onion and Parmesan on top.
- Mix the remaining 2 tablespoons of olive oil and lemon juice in a medium bowl. Serve spinach salad with vinaigrette beside the omelet.

Nutritional facts
- Calories: 330
- Carbs: 6g
- Fat: 27.5g
- Protein: 16g

2. **Scrambled eggs**
   - Preparation time: 5 minutes
   - Cooking time: 15 minutes
   - Serving: 4

Ingredients
   - 8 eggs
   - ¼ teaspoon of salt
   - 1-2 tablespoons of butter
   - ½ cup of milk
   - ½ cup bell peppers, chopped
   - ½ (small) onion diced
   - 3/4 cup mushrooms, sliced
   - 4 cooked bacon slices, chopped
   - 2 Roma tomatoes chopped
   - ½ cup cheddar cheese, shredded
   - Chopped chives

Directions
   - Combine the egg, milk, and salt in a large bowl and whisk together. Place aside.
   - In a big skillet, melt the butter over medium heat. Add the mushrooms, bell peppers, onion, and a dash of salt when the mixture has heated. Cook until softened for a few minutes. Add the bacon and tomatoes after that.
   - The egg mixture into the pan. As desired, gently scramble the eggs. Cheese and chives should be added on top.

Nutritional facts
   - Calories: 285
   - Carbs: 7g
   - Fat: 20g
   - Protein: 19g

3. **Sun-dried eggs**
   - Preparation time: 1 minute
   - Cooking time: 2 minutes
   - Serving: 4

Ingredients
   - 4 large-size eggs
   - 1 tablespoon vegetable oil
   - 1 (large) bell pepper
   - parsley, chopped for garnish

Directions
   - Remove the white flesh and seeds from bell peppers and cut each pepper in half horizontally to produce four 1/2-inch-thick rings.

- Heat vegetable oil over medium heat in a 12-inch nonstick skillet. Cook peppers for two minutes. Crack one egg into the center of each pepper ring after turning them over.
- Cook eggs under cover until they are the desired doneness. Add a quarter teaspoon of each pepper and salt.
- Garnish each serving with chopped parsley.

Nutritional facts
- Calories: 215
- Carbs: 3g
- Fat: 17g
- Protein: 13g

4. Egg and chicken sandwich
- Preparation time: 5 minutes
- Cooking time: 30 minutes
- Serving: 4

Ingredients
- ¼ cup of mayonnaise
- 1 teaspoon of olive oil
- 2 teaspoons lemon zest, grated + 2 tablespoons juice
- 1 (small) garlic clove, grated
- 4 (bone-in, skin-on) chicken thighs
- 4 slices of rustic bread, toasted
- 1 tomato, sliced
- 4 large-size eggs
- ½ cup of fresh parsley
- pepper and coarse salt

Directions
- Stir garlic and mayonnaise in a small bowl. Add salt and pepper to taste on the bread, and spread. Remove the bone from each chicken thigh while leaving the skin on with a paring knife.
- Oil should be heated over medium-high in a sizable nonstick skillet. Cook chicken with seasoning, skin-side down, for about 6 minutes or until the skin turns golden brown.
- About 4 minutes after flipping, the chicken should be fully cooked. Put the chicken in a dish and add some lemon juice.
- Add eggs to the skillet and lower the heat to medium. About 3 minutes of cooking time is required to get the whites set and the yolks runny.
- Sandwiches can be made by assembling bread, egg, chicken, tomato, and parsley.

Nutritional facts

- Calories: 215
- Carbs: 3g
- Fat: 17g
- Protein: 13g

5. <u>Avocado baked egg</u>

- Preparation time: 8 minutes
- Cooking time: 12 minutes
- Serving: 6

Ingredients

- 6 (large) eggs
- ¼ cup of cheddar cheese
- 2 tablespoons chives, sliced thinly
- 2 tablespoons (red) bell peppers, diced finely
- 3 large-size avocados
- black pepper
- sea salt

Directions

- Set the oven's temperature to 400 °F (204 °C).
- Remove the avocados' pits and half them. Create a well big enough to hold an egg in the center of the avocado by spooning 1.5–2 teaspoons (2–28 g) of the flesh out. A total of around 3 teaspoons (42 g) must fit in the well.
- Put the cut-side-up avocado halves on a baking sheet. Place an egg in the middle of each, taking care not to crack the yolk.
- Add some black pepper and sea salt.
- For 7 minutes, bake. Add some cheese shavings on top. Bake the eggs for a further 5 to 10 minutes, depending on how done you like them.
- For serving, top with chopped chives and bell peppers.

Nutritional facts

- Calories: 254
- Carbs: 9g
- Fat: 21g
- Protein: 10g

6. <u>Chicken wings</u>

- Preparation time: 20 minutes
- Cooking time: 3 hours
- Serving: 40 pieces

Ingredients

- 4 pounds of chicken wings
- 1 cup of soy sauce
- 1 tablespoon of sesame seeds

- o 1 cup of barbecue sauce
- o 6 (green) onions, chopped and divided

Directions

Cut through each wing's two joints with a sharp knife; throw away wing tips. In a 4- or 5-qt slow cooker, add the remaining wing pieces. Stir in 1/4 cup finely chopped green onions, soy sauce, and barbecue sauce. Cook covered for 3–4 hours on high or until tender. Sprinkle with the leftover green onions and sesame seeds.

Nutritional facts

- o Calories: 68
- o Carbs: 3g
- o Fat: 4g
- o Protein: 6g

7. Garlic-soy chicken

- o Preparation time: 10 minutes
- o Cooking time: 4 hours
- o Serving: 6

Ingredients

- o 6 skinless chicken leg quarters
- o ¼ cup brown sugar, packed
- o ½ cup soy sauce, reduced-sodium
- o 2 teaspoons garlic, minced
- o 1 can (8 ounces) of tomato sauce

Directions

- o Leg quarters can optionally be sliced at the joints with a sharp knife. Place in a 4-quart slow cooker. Mix the garlic, tomato sauce, brown sugar, and soy sauce in a small bowl; pour over the chicken.
- o Chicken should be tender after 4–5 hours of cooking on low with the cover on.

Nutritional facts

- o Calories: 246
- o Carbs: 13g
- o Fat: 2g
- o Protein: 29g

8. Chicken adobo

- o Preparation time: 10 minutes
- o Cooking time: 30 minutes
- o Serving: 4

Ingredients

- o 6 (bone-in, skinless) chicken thighs
- o 1 tablespoon of vegetable oil
- o ⅔ cup apple cider vinegar
- o 3 cloves of garlic, minced
- o ⅓ cup of soy sauce
- o 1 bay leaf

- o 1 teaspoon of black peppercorns, whole

Directions

- o In a medium frying pan, heat the oil over medium-high heat. About 5 minutes after adding the chicken, grill it on the other side for a further 5 minutes or until it is just lightly browned. Place the chicken on a platter and reserve.
- o Then, put the pan back on low heat after draining all but 1 tablespoon of the drippings. Add the garlic and cook for approximately a minute or until soft. Stir in the remaining ingredients after adding them. Cook the chicken in the pan once more for 20 minutes with the lid on.
- o Remove the cover, lower the heat to medium-low, and simmer the chicken for a further 15 to 20 minutes, spooning sauce over it occasionally, until it is cooked and well-glazed with sauce and the sauce has slightly thickened. Before eating, remove the bay leaf.

Nutritional facts

- o Calories: 254
- o Carbs: 5g
- o Fat: 9g
- o Protein: 34g

9. **Chicken cheese soup**

- o Preparation time: 5 minutes
- o Cooking time: 30 minutes
- o Serving: 8

Ingredients

- o 4 cups cooked chicken breast, shredded
- o 1 package (16 ounces) of mixed vegetables, frozen and thawed
- o 2 cans (10-3/4 ounces each) chicken soup-condensed cream, undiluted
- o 1 pound Velveeta, cubed
- o 1 can (14-1/2 ounces) potatoes, diced and drained
- o 3-1/2 cups of water
- o chives, minced (optional)

Directions

- o Combine the first five ingredients in a Dutch oven up to a boil. Reduce heat, cover, and simmer for 8 to 10 minutes or until vegetables are soft. Cheese should only be stirred in briefly, not boiled. Add fresh chives minced on top if you like.

Nutritional facts

- Calories: 429
- Carbs: 23g
- Fat: 22g
- Protein: 33g

10. Fried chicken rice

- Preparation time: 5 minutes
- Cooking time: 30 minutes
- Serving: 6

Ingredients

- 1 package (12 ounces) of mixed vegetables, frozen
- 2 tablespoons of olive oil, divided
- 4 tablespoons of sesame oil, divided
- 1 rotisserie chicken, skinless and shredded
- 3 packages (8.8 ounces each) of vegetable rice, ready-to-serve
- ¼ teaspoon of pepper
- ¼ teaspoon of salt

Directions

- Prepare frozen vegetables as directed on the package. In the meantime, warm 1 tablespoon of olive oil to medium-high heat in a big skillet. Pour in the eggs, then heat and whisk them until there is no longer any liquid egg. Take out of the pan.
- Heat the remaining 1 tablespoon of olive oil and 2 tablespoons of sesame oil in the same skillet over medium-high heat. Add the rice; simmer and stir for 10–12 minutes or until the rice starts to brown.
- Chicken, salt, and pepper are stirred in. Vegetables and eggs are then heated through while eggs are broken into tiny bits and combined. Add the final 2 teaspoons of sesame oil.

Nutritional facts

- Calories: 548
- Carbs: 43g
- Fat: 25g
- Protein: 38g

7.3 Keeping eggs and meat fresh for future use

It's critical to properly store eggs and meat in order to preserve their freshness and safety for usage in the future. The following are some general recommendations for storing eggs:

- Eggs should be stored in their original carton within the refrigerator's primary compartment, not in the door, where the temperature fluctuates frequently.
- Because eggs can absorb flavors, keep them away from foods with strong aromas.
- In the refrigerator, eggs can be kept for up to four to five weeks.

Following are some general recommendations for storing hens' meat:

- To prevent cross-contamination, always keep raw meat in another container or on a different shelf in the refrigerator.
- To cut down bacterial growth, keep your refrigerator at or below 40°F (4°C).
- If you won't use the meat within a few days, freeze it.
- Before freezing, cover meat tightly with plastic wrap, aluminum foil, or a container with a tight-fitting lid.
- Use within the prescribed storage times for every type of meat, and mark each package with the date and permanent marker.

7.4 Producing fertilizer for the home garden

The health and production of your kitchen garden can be increased in a cost-efficient and ecologically responsible manner by using chicken dung as fertilizer. The growth and development of plants depend on elements like potassium, phosphorus, and nitrogen, which are abundant in chicken manure. In my response, I'll describe how to make chicken dung as fertilizer and its advantages for the environment and gardens.

Creating chicken excrement for use as fertilizer:

1. Gather chicken poop
2. Composting the manure entails using bacteria and other microbes to break down the organic material in the manure.
3. A few months are typically needed for the composting process to be

complete. The compost will be crumbly, black, and earthy when it is finished. This shows that it is nutrient-rich and ready to be used as fertilizer.

The use of chicken manure as fertilizer for gardens and the environment has numerous positive effects:

- Provides vital nutrients for plant growth and development, including the elements phosphorus, nitrogen, and potassium.

- Enhances soil fertility and water-holding capacity as well as soil structure. This can enhance drainage, stop soil erosion, and use less water.

- One efficient method of recycling organic waste is to use chicken dung as fertilizer. By doing this, less waste ends up in landfills, which can release toxic gases and fuel climate change.

- By utilizing chicken dung as fertilizer, you may save money on fertilizers and soil additives while enhancing the health and production of your garden.

Conclusion

You must be realistic while dealing with chickens. Animals are not commodities that can be dumped when their owners change their minds, so be sure you're ready for the commitment. Make sure you are prepared for the commitment before you start because rehoming birds is more difficult than rehoming other pets.

Hens are not the foolish birds that are commonly portrayed, which makes a living with them eye-opening. They're able to distinguish between well over a hundred individual chickens and humans, have a robust vocabulary and have good memories.

This book offers advice on how to make sure your hens produce eggs of the highest caliber. Learn how to avoid the repercussions of a poorly cared-for family by adopting a natural, artificial-free lifestyle that is in tune with the environment and addresses long-term health and preventative maintenance concerns.

You'll gain knowledge on how to handle predators. The discovery that an animal has burgled your yard or coop and killed your hens is the most heartbreaking thing you can imagine. It will discuss ailments, parasites, and other issues that all chicken owners deal with. Your flock may become overrun by lice, mites, and other bugs, or an invasive rat may carry undesirable pests with it.

If you follow the advice in this detailed manual, you'll be able to provide a safe and healthy environment for your chickens while also reaping the benefits of a more locally sourced and environmentally friendly diet. You may easily become a prosperous chicken keeper and take advantage of the many advantages that come with it with a little perseverance, effort, and dedication. So why not start growing chickens right away and give it a shot?

Made in United States
Troutdale, OR
06/07/2023

10493567R00035